CW00547353

Delaney
Street
Press

The Golfer's Book
of Inspiration

The Golfer's Book
of Inspiration

By Criswell Freeman

DELANEY STREET PRESS
Nashville, TN; Telephone: (800)-256-8584

ISBN 1-58334-071-8

The ideas expressed in this book are not, in all cases, exact quotations, as some have been edited for clarity and brevity. In all cases, the author has attempted to maintain the speaker's original intent. In some cases, material for this book was obtained from secondary sources, primarily print media. While every effort was made to ensure the accuracy of these sources, the accuracy cannot be guaranteed. For additions, deletions, corrections or clarifications in future editions of this text, please write DELANEY STREET PRESS.

Printed in the United States of America
Cover Design by Bart Dawson
Typesetting & Page Layout by Sue Gerdes
Editor for Delaney Street Press: Alan Ross
1 2 3 4 5 6 7 8 9 10 • 00 01 02 03 04 05 06

ACKNOWLEDGMENTS
The author gratefully acknowledges the helpful support of the staff of Walnut Grove Press and Delaney Street Press.

For Tom Gildemeister

Table of Contents

Introduction

Golf is a mental exercise. Clear thinking and sound judgement are as much a part of the game as tee boxes and sand traps. Success on the links requires preparation, patience, self-control, concentration, and positive thinking. Golfers who possess these attributes win tournaments; golfers who lack them don't.

Every golfer, no matter how experienced, can benefit from a refresher course in the mental aspects of the game. This book is intended as a concise summary of golf's most important principles, as told by the some of the game's greatest players.

The better part of golf is played between the ears, so players of all ages and handicaps are advised to pay close attention to the ideas that follow. The careful reader will discover that the game of golf is much more than an exercise in swinging a club and striking a little white ball. Golf is an exercise in positive thinking, as the following collection of quotations will attest.

1

The Greatest Game

What makes golf the greatest game? Many things. Golf is a pleasing combination of physical exercise and mental concentration. It provides the golfer with time and opportunity to walk over God's green earth and to enjoy Mother Nature in all her splendor. Golf is also a social game, the perfect place to renew old friendships and make new ones.

The game of golf meets a player's innate need for competition, both with others and with himself. The more a golfer works at the game, the more he or she improves. With improvement, however gradual, comes a feeling of satisfaction and accomplishment.

Golf, by its very nature, is a quiet game, giving thoughtful players ample time to reflect on matters beyond the 18th green. It is no surprise, then, that the golf course is a crucible of learning, a place where self-discipline is revered and rewarded.

What is golf? It is many things, but first and foremost, golf is perhaps the most perfect game yet invented by man.

No other game combines the wonder
of nature with the discipline of sport
in such carefully planned ways.
A great golf course both frees and
challenges a golfer's mind.

Tom Watson

Golf is deceptively simple
yet endlessly complicated.

Arnold Palmer

Golf is a game in which perfection
stays just out of reach.

Betsy Rawls

Golf is a day spent in
a round of strenuous
idleness.

William Wordsworth

Golf has probably
kept more people sane
than psychiatrists have.

Harvey Penick

Golf is a great and glorious game.
Even those of us who earn our livings
at it play it more for the pleasure
than for the money.
Arnold Palmer

Take pleasure not in the score,
but in the game.
Bobby Jones

Playing golf is a privilege,
not a sentence.
Harvey Penick

Golf is a lot like life.
It will test your patience. It will dazzle
and baffle you with highs and lows,
successes and frustrations.

Amy Alcott

Golf is the most human game of all.
You have all the highs and lows —
sometimes in the same round.

Lee Trevino

Golf is the "only-est" sport. You're
completely alone with every opportunity
to defeat yourself.

Hale Irwin

Golf is going to test you, but the test
is only a game.

Tom Watson

Golf acts as a corrective
against sinful pride.

P. G. Wodehouse

In golf, while there is life, there is hope.

Walter Simpson

I played many sports,
but when the
golf bug bit me,
it was permanent.

Babe Didrikson Zaharias

Golf is an ideal
diversion but
a ruinous disease.

B. C. Forbes

If the sun is up,
why aren't you
playing golf?

Lee Trevino

2

Attitude

On the links, the self-fulfilling prophecy is alive and well: Confident golf is good golf, while hesitant golf is high-handicap golf. Thus the attitude with which a player approaches the game determines, in large part, success or failure. The quotations on the following pages are designed to raise confidence levels and lower handicaps.

There's absolutely no question that golf is a game of mind over matter.

Gary Player

I think that to score in golf
is a matter of confidence.

Henry Cotton

In my opinion, the average golfer
underestimates himself.

Ben Hogan

You have more potential than you think.

Sam Snead

The philosophy
of "think positive"
is essential for
winning golf.

Nancy Lopez

You are what
you think you are
in golf and in life.
Raymond Floyd

I'm as good a player as I think I am.
If you can't win in your dreams, forget it.
Calvin Peete

My father told me, "You must never
learn to think the negative."
Johnny Miller

Don't linger too long in thinking about
your shots — good or bad — but stamp
the good ones into your mind
for future reference.
Greg Norman

Never think about what you did wrong
on the last shot. Think about what you
will do right on the next one.
Tommy Armour

The more time I have to think about
a shot, the worse I'm going to hit it.
Larry Laoretti

If a player is confident in a club he has
selected, that confidence is reflected
in his swing.
Cary Middlecoff

Imagine what you want to do,
   not what you don't want to do.
                              Sandra Haynie

Practice your swing until it becomes
   a habit of mind and muscle.
                              Sam Snead

Make up your mind before your
backswing starts, then let your muscles
         do the work.
                              Tommy Armour

Do your best, one shot at a time, and then move on. Remember that golf is just a game.

Nancy Lopez

There is no room on the golf course
for anger or self-pity.

Greg Norman

Great players concentrate on cause
rather than result.

Cary Middlecoff

Golf is a game of misses, and the winners
are those who have the best misses.

Kathy Whitworth

The most important thing for me in preparing for a major tournament is basic peace of mind.

Jack Nicklaus

Golf is 20% mechanics
and technique.
The other 80%
is philosophy, humor,
tragedy, romance,
melodrama,
companionship,
camaraderie,
cussedness, and
conversation.

Grantland Rice

3

Concentration

The game of golf requires concentration: The player whose mind wanders far and wide is the player whose shots do likewise. Conversely, the player who learns to focus his thoughts is rewarded with a low handicap and a full trophy case. Therefore, players who wish to improve their scores must first learn to improve their powers of concentration. The following quotations tell how.

On the golf course,
concentrate on the
present, forget the past,
and don't look
too far ahead.

Judy Rankin

Maintaining composure on the golf course is worth at least three shots a round.

Billy Casper

Some golfers I've :met can't achieve
total concentration because they're
too brilliant for their own good.
They over-analyze.

Sam Snead

The difference between ordinary players
and champions is the way they think.

Patty Berg

Golf is you against yourself.

Jack Nicklaus

Focus not on the commotion around you but on the opportunity ahead of you.

Arnold Palmer

Most golfers prepare for disaster.
A good golfer prepares for success.
Bob Toski

The more patience you have, the better
you play.
Colleen Walker

You tend to get impatient with
less-than-perfect shots, but you have
to remember that less-than-perfect shots
win Opens.
Curtis Strange

Don't be in such a hurry. That little white ball isn't going to run away from you.

Patty Berg

Keep your head down, don't visit with anyone during the round, and go about your business.

Ben Hogan

4

Course Management

Patty Sheehan was once asked to describe what course management meant to her. She responded, "Course management means you are in control of the golf course rather than vice versa." Unfortunately, this kind of mastery is easier said than done — fortunately, it *is* possible.

Golf is a next-shot game, one that is best played with forethought and discernment. Top players manage the course — and themselves — with this thought in mind.

Be yourself.
Play within yourself.
Play your own game.
Harvey Penick

Play your own game.
You can't be something
you're not.

David Duval

Don't just play your way
around the course.
Think your way
around the course.

Sam Snead

The key to golf is to play the ball
to the best position from which to play
the next shot.

Arnold Palmer

Course management is like being
in a chess game. You're maneuvering
for position.

Patty Sheehan

The best strategic advice is this:
Know your strengths and take advantage
of them.

Greg Norman

Play the shot you've got the best chance
of playing well.

Greg Norman

Don't be ashamed to play safe.

Arnold Palmer

There's no rule in golf that states,
"Thou shalt shoot for the flagstick."

Patty Sheehan

One of the worst mistakes you can make in golf is trying to force the game.

Jack Nicklaus

Play away from trouble.
> *Babe Didrikson Zaharias*

I have seen many good players
attempt shots they should have known
were impossible.
> *Bobby Jones*

Never let one bad shot disrupt
your rhythm or concentration.
> *Sam Snead*

Missing a short putt
doesn't mean that I
have to hit my next shot
out of bounds.

Tony Lema

You can't get too keyed up
about the bounces a golf ball takes.

Greg Norman

Good breaks and bad breaks are part
of the game. You just learn to take
both in stride.

Tiger Woods

The game isn't fair,
but then life isn't fair either.

Lee Trevino

You don't have to hit the ball perfectly to win. You just have to manage yourself better.

Tom Watson

The object of golf
is to beat someone.
Make sure that someone
is not yourself.

Bobby Jones

5

Preparation

Golf requires scrupulous preparation. Inevitably, the game favors intense, meticulous preparation over natural talent. The player who decides, with firm resolve, to improve his or her game will, over time, see results. But the player who is unwilling to invest energy on the practice tee must be willing to settle for perpetual mediocrity on the links.

The following quotations serve as guideposts on the way to better golf. May they inspire you to improve *your* game.

I try to learn from everyone.
I look at their strengths and ask myself,
"What can I do better."
Annika Sorenstam

I'm still learning how to play the game.
I recognize that.
Tiger Woods

You never stop learning in this sport.
Once you think you've got one part of
the game licked, another one goes.
Dinah Shore

Golf is a game
of finding what works,
losing it, and then
finding it again.

Ken Venturi

The reason for my success is simple.
15 years of practice and hard work.
David Duval

You can't go into a golf shop and
buy a good game.
Sam Snead

The world took six days. Your golf swing
may take a little longer.
Glen Waggoner

There's nothing in the game of golf
that can't be improved upon —
if you practice.

Patty Berg

The way to build your swing is through
intelligent practice.

Cary Middlecoff

There's much more to learning how
to hit good golf shots than belting out
a few million balls.

Jack Nicklaus

Correct instruction and lots of practice:
That's my winning combination.
Babe Didrikson Zaharias

Correct one fault at a time.
Concentrate on the one fault
that you want to overcome.
Sam Snead

When practicing, use the club that
gives you the most trouble, not the one
that gives you the most satisfaction.
Harry Vardon

The most common practice error
is to drift aimlessly to the range and
start banging balls at random.

Tony Lema

Never practice without a thought
in mind.

Nancy Lopez

Every time you go out to hit a bucket
of balls, it should be
with a definite purpose.

Dow Finsterwald

Make a game out of practice. You're still a child at heart.

Harvey Penick

Always keep learning.
It keeps you young.

Patty Berg

You find talent not by looking for it
but by working for it.
Nancy Lopez

Don't be too anxious to see good results
on the scoreboard until you have fully
absorbed the principles of the golf swing
on the practice tee.
Louise Suggs

A couple of hours of practice
is worth ten sloppy rounds.
Babe Didrikson Zaharias

You must work
very hard to become
a natural golfer.

Gary Player

Never be afraid to take
a lesson. I'm not.
Jack Nicklaus

6

Adversity

On the golf course, trouble is only a swing away. Every course has its share of hazards, traps, and obstacles. The golfer's challenge is simple: avoid adversity. But steering clear of misfortune for an entire 18 holes is impossible, so every player in every round must deal with slices, hooks, bad bounces and lipped-out putts. In this chapter, a cross section of history's greatest golfers share valuable advice for overcoming adversity. Feel free to use these tips on the course or off.

When you're playing poorly, you start
thinking too much. That's when
you confuse yourself.

Greg Norman

Thinking instead of acting
is the number one disease in golf.

Sam Snead

The secret of playing well is to find
your comfort level, play smart,
and avoid mistakes.

David Duval

Start each hole with an awareness
   that there may be subtle or mysterious
elements waiting to sabotage your game.
                              Robert Trent Jones, Jr.

One bad shot does not make
            a losing score.
                                    Gay Brewer

Every golfer can expect to have four
      bad shots a round. When you do,
         just put them out of your mind.
                                    Walter Hagen

Adversity is a fork in the road. You'll get better or you'll get worse, but you'll never be the same.

Ken Venturi

Good golfers learn
to convert anger
into productivity.

Tommy Bolt

When in trouble, play the shot you
know you can play, not the shot you hope
you can play.
Jack Burke, Jr.

Every great player has learned
the two C's: How to *concentrate*
and how to maintain *composure*.
Byron Nelson

Only long practice and the ability
to think under pressure will enable you
to hit the ball out of trouble under
tough circumstances and prevent you
from beating yourself.
Babe Didrikson Zaharias

Anger has no place on the course. All it does is hurt you.

Sally Little

No matter what
happens, keep hitting
the ball.

Harry Vardon

7

Self-Control

Players who seek to win championships must first learn to control their emotions. Serious golfers recognize that temper tantrums and angry outbursts have no place on the course. Anger has never won a golf tournament.

Some golfers never gain a meaningful measure of self-mastery; these unfortunate players never reach their full potential. But the best golfers learn to bridle their frustrations and focus their minds on the task at hand. In doing so, these disciplined players improve not only their scores but also their lives.

More than any other game, golf is
about self-control, restraint of personality,
and the mastering of emotions.
Thomas Boswell

Being in control on a golf course means
making intelligent decisions —
knowing when to be aggressive
and when to be cautious.
Curtis Strange

Over-aggression has never won
a golf tournament.
Jack Nicklaus

A lot of times,
you don't actually win
so much as the other
guys lose.

Jack Nicklaus

Dare to play your
own game.
Annika Sorenstam

Live your own life
and play up to your own
expectations, on the
course or off.

Tiger Woods

Mental discipline, muscle memory.
Practice until you don't have to think.
Calvin Peete

Tension is golf's worst enemy.
Bobby Jones

I don't go into a trance when I address
the ball, but I come close.
Sam Snead

If you have discipline, you can relax
and concentrate.

Sandra Haynie

We create success or failure on the
course primarily through our thoughts.

Gary Player

The difference between winning and
losing is always a mental one.

Peter Thomson

Golf is more
in your mind than
in your clubs.

Bruce Crampton

8

Putting

Putting separates greats from near-greats, champions from runners-up, and low handicappers from duffers. The putting stroke is, ironically, the least powerful shot in a golfer's repertoire *and* the most important. Seasoned veterans understand all too well that the secret of winning golf is often nothing more than the ability to sink a string of testy five-footers.

In this chapter, the game's greatest golfers reveal some of their most powerful putting pointers. The following quotations underscore the old golf adage: "Drive for show and putt for dough." All those who wish to lower their handicaps had best pay close attention ... and make a few testy five-footers.

One of the main reasons for my putting success is that I've always tried to keep my method simple.

Ben Crenshaw

All good putters have balance.

Arnold Palmer

Good putters keep their bodies still during the stroke.

Gary Player

A firm stroke is a good stroke.

Greg Norman

All good putters hit the ball solidly.

Cary Middlecoff

Consistent putts stem from consistent,
solid strikes on the middle
of the clubface.

Ben Crenshaw

Good putters don't raise their heads
until the ball is partway along the line
to the cup.

Cary Middlecoff

Seven out of ten times I hit a bad putt,
it's because I was too eager to see what
happened to the ball. Don't be so anxious
to see the results...stay down
through the putt.

Ben Crenshaw

The most important element of good putting is the ability to concentrate on the problem at hand.

Bobby Jones

If I had my early life to live over,
I would practice my putting
twice as much as I did.
Gary Player

Practice three- and four-footers twice as
much as you practice long putts.
Billy Casper

Mr. Average Golfer spends too much
time tinkering with his long game
at the expense of the short.
Ian Woosnam

The standout putters on the tour are the guys who wear grooves in practice greens and motel rugs.

Gay Brewer

Begin by practicing the short putts first.

Billy Casper

Never lose the will to improve.

Tom Watson

Any player's putting
skill on a given day
is in direct ratio to his
confidence on that day.

Cary Middlecoff

Great champions make big putts.

Phil Mickelson

Keep a carefree attitude about your putting. Do the best you can on every stroke, then take an accepting attitude toward the results.

Fred Couples

Let God's hand rest on your shoulder, and if it's your turn to win, you will win.

Harvey Penick

Don't be a negative putter.

Billy Casper

You can tell a good putt
by the noise it makes.

Bobby Locke

9

The Joy of Golf

Mark Twain once observed, "Golf is a good walk spoiled." Nothing could be further from the truth. In actuality, golf is a good walk vastly improved, and observant players are quick to appreciate the improvements.

The golf course should be a place of inspiration, not frustration. Thus savvy players don't forget that "teeing it up" is a privilege, one that should never be squandered in fits of anger or darkened by clouds of regret. Golf, even on a day when birdies are scarce and bogies are plentiful, is an opportunity to experience one of life's grand pleasures. So why not enjoy every single round?

A round of golf should permit 18 inspirations.

A. W. Tillinghast

Try to find something joyful about each round of golf.

Patty Sheehan

Play happy.

Domingo Lopez (Nancy's father)

I believe golf can bring you happiness.

Harvey Penick

You can think best when you're happiest.

Peter Thomson

Enjoy the game.
Happy golf is good golf.
Gary Player

Go out and have fun.
Golf is a game for
everyone, not just for
the talented few.

Harvey Penick

My positive thinking starts on the tee.
Sandra Haynie

Give it your best, but always with the knowledge that your happiness and your livelihood are not riding on the next shot.
Jane Blalock

Don't take your bad shots home with you.

Tony Lema

Don't hurry. Don't
worry. You're only
here for a short visit.
So don't forget to stop
and smell the roses.

Walter Hagen

10

All-Purpose Advice

We conclude with a potpourri of timeless wisdom from some of the game's greatest players. Enjoy. And happy golfing!

The man who says his knees aren't shaking as he stands over a this-to-win putt is lying.

Ian Woosnam

Every time you have a chance to win, you get nervous, but I like that. I'd rather be nervous and tense teeing off Sunday afternoon than be calm and teeing off at 9:00 on Sunday morning.

David Duval

The simpler the stroke,
the more effective it is
under pressure.

Billy Casper

To be consistently effective, you must
put a certain distance between yourself
and what happens to you
on the golf course.

Sam Snead

Take it easy on yourself
when you miss one.

Arnold Palmer

Realize that even with the short ones,
you can't make them all.

Curtis Strange

Remember that
golf presents
no physical danger.

Bobby Jones

Be decisive.
A wrong decision is
generally less disastrous
than indecision.

Bernhard Langer

What kind of putter is best? The one in the most confident hands.

Bob Rosburg

Little good comes
from brooding about
mistakes. The next shot,
in golf or in life,
is the big one.

Grantland Rice

Nobody has enough natural ability
to become a real champion. You've got
to know the fundamentals of the game
to get up there and stay up there.
Gary Player

Be patient. Acquiring finesse takes time.
Amy Alcott

Repetition is the key to good habits,
in golf and in life.
Sandra Haynie

Golf, like measles,
    should be caught young.
P. G. Wodehouse

Nothing goes down slower
    than a golf handicap.
Bobby Nichols

You never master golf. You take what
    it gives, and you learn from it.
Charlie Sifford

Golfers have analyzed
the game in order
to find "the secret."
There is no secret.

Henry Cotton

You're never too old
to play golf. If you can
walk, you can play.

Louise Suggs

When I'm off the course, I know how old I am. When I'm on the course, I'm a kid again.

JoAnne Carner

Always use a clean ball.
Harry Vardon

In choosing a partner,
always pick
the optimist.

Tony Lema

I can sum it up
like this: thank God
for the game of golf.
Arnold Palmer

Sources

About
DELANEY STREET PRESS

DELANEY STREET PRESS publishes books designed to inspire and entertain readers of all ages. DELANEY STREET books are distributed by Walnut Grove Press. For more information, call 1-800-256-8584.

About the Author

Criswell Freeman is a Doctor of Clinical Psychology living in Nashville, Tennessee. In addition to this text, Dr. Freeman has compiled several golf quotation books, along with numerous other titles published by Walnut Grove Press. He is also the author of a bestselling self-help book entitled *When Life Throws You a Curveball, Hit It.*